COMPUTER ANIMATION

Cavendish
Square
New York

Cathleen
Small

For Chris, who doesn't laugh at me when I bawl during Up.
Thanks for being the Carl to my Ellie.

Published in 2015 by Cavendish Square Publishing, LLC
243 5th Avenue, Suite 136, New York, NY 10016

First Edition

Website: cavendishsq.com

This publication represents the opinions and views of the author based on his or her personal experience,
knowledge, and research. The information in this book serves as a general guide only. The author and
publisher have used their best efforts in preparing this book and disclaim liability rising directly or
indirectly from the use and application of this book.

CPSIA Compliance Information: Batch #WW15CSQ

All websites were available and accurate when this book was sent to press.

Library of Congress Cataloging-in-Publication Data

Small, Cathleen, author.
Computer animation / Cathleen Small.
pages cm. — (High-tech jobs)
Includes bibliographical references and index.
ISBN 978-1-50260-106-3 (hardcover) ISBN 978-1-50260-107-0 (ebook)
1. Computer animation—Vocational guidance—Juvenile literature. 2. Computer graphics—Vocational
guidance—Juvenile literature. I. Title.

TR897.7.S63 2015
006.6'96'023—dc23

2014028065

Editor: Kristen Susienka
Copy Editor: Cynthia Roby
Art Director: Jeffrey Talbot
Senior Designer: Amy Greenan
Senior Production Manager: Jennifer Ryder-Talbot
Production Editor: David McNamara
Photo Researcher: J8 Media

Printed in the United States of America

CONTENTS

Disney's *Frozen* is a wildly successful example of computer animation in film.

INTRODUCTION TO COMPUTER ANIMATION

T oy Story. Frozen. Pixar. Transformers. Halo. Industrial Light & Magic. Auto manufacturers. Advertising agencies. Pharmaceutical companies. Bloggers. What do all of these things have in common? They are all films, video games, or companies that use computer animation. Some undoubtedly didn't surprise you. Nearly everyone knows Toy Story and Frozen are animated films, and you might've even been aware that Transformers used computer animation for much of the movie. Halo is a popular video game, and Pixar—when you think animation, you think Pixar—but did the last four surprise you at all? They shouldn't, because computer animation is everywhere.

Auto manufacturers use computer animation to help them work out new features on various car models. Ad agencies use animation all the time when creating television advertisements for products. Pharmaceutical companies use computer animation

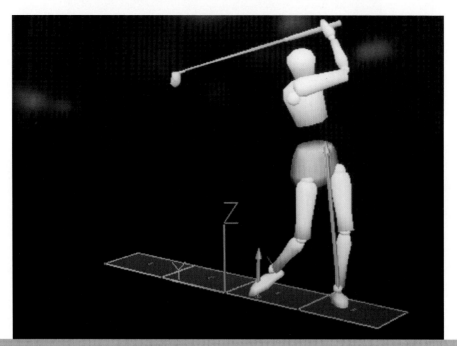

Many industries use computer animation to create simulations.

to create medical **simulations** and to illustrate how a certain treatment will affect a patient's body. Even everyday bloggers can use computer animation to create quick animated snippets known as animated GIFs (discussed later in this book). First, let's define computer animation.

WHAT IS COMPUTER ANIMATION?

Most simply put, computer animation is the art and science of using computers to create moving images. These moving images can be obvious animations, such as the machines in *Transformers*, or they can be so subtle and realistic that they blend seamlessly with real actors in films, such as when animation is used to create realistic moving backgrounds for films.

There are numerous types of computer animation, which we'll cover in more depth later in this book. You'll learn about 2-D and

3-D animation, **stop-motion**, **CGI**, and claymation. Since the computer animation industry has been so successful for many years, there are several tools available to help computer animators create their content. We'll discuss some of the software packages later in this book, too. Some are quite expensive and complicated to learn, but others are fairly inexpensive and something you can play around with at home to learn the basics of animating with that software package.

ART AND SCIENCE

More than many other careers, computer animation is truly both an art and a science. You must have a logic-driven, scientific side to understand how to use the computer to help you create animations, but you must also have an artistic sensibility because, at its core, animation is artwork. The principles of design and **aesthetics**, or beauty, still apply, even though the art is being created with the use of a computer.

Worried that your scientific side outweighs your artistic side, or vice versa? Don't be. The field of computer animation offers a number of viable career paths, and some are more on the technical side of things, while others focus more on the artistic side. If you have some level of artistic talent and are technically **savvy**, and interested in computer animation, rest assured that there's a career there for you.

THE EVOLUTION OF COMPUTER ANIMATION

The true beginning of computer animation varies depending on what you consider animation and what you consider a computer. Some people consider machines such as the **zoetrope** from the early 1800s to be rudimentary computers that created animation. However, most people in the field agree that true computer animation, as we know it, began in the late 1950s and early 1960s.

John Whitney, Sr. was a pioneer in computer animation. Along with his brother, James, he created experimental film

animations in the 1940s and 1950s. In 1958, he helped create the animated title sequence for the Alfred Hitchcock film *Vertigo*. Whitney established the company Motion Graphics Inc. and is perhaps best known for pioneering an animation effect, motion control model photography, that was used in the groundbreaking film *2001: A Space Odyssey*.

Although important to the history of computer animation, Whitney was far from the only contributor. Bell Labs in New Jersey was a big part of the field from the early 1960s, employing several pioneering computer animators who developed techniques crucial to early computer animation.

William Fetter of Boeing developed the first 3-D animated wireframe human figures in the 1960s, a technique that is still widely used today. Nikolai Konstantinov and a team from the Soviet Union created one of the first computer animations of an actual character—a cat that walked—in 1968. The animated feline was rudimentary but groundbreaking.

Another animation pioneer was Ivan Sutherland from MIT. Sutherland developed the first **graphical user interface**, a critical component in not just computer animation but computer platforms as a whole today. The graphical user interface (or GUI, as it is commonly called) changed the face of computers, quite literally, in fact. People went from staring at lines of code to accomplish simple computer tasks to seeing a simple, user-friendly interface that even novice computer users could easily navigate. For computer animators, the GUI is critical, as they can see and manipulate their artistic images on the screen.

Earlier, you read about 2-D and 3-D animation, which you'll learn more about later in this book. One thing to note, however, is that 3-D animation became much more widespread in the 1970s, after a number of pioneering achievements in graphics at the University of Utah. The 1960s and 1970s were a time of fast-and-furious developments in computer animation. In 1977 the use of 3-D computer graphics in film was debuted in the movie *Star Wars: Episode IV: A New Hope*. In the movie, Luke Skywalker and the rebel pilots used a 3-D wireframe view of the Death Star's trench to hit the exhaust port, the Death Star's weak point. That was achieved with 3-D computer graphics. Many people think *TRON* (1982) was the first movie to use computer graphics, but in reality *TRON* was predated by *Star Wars* (1977), *Alien* (1979), and *Looker* (1981).

From then on, digital animation exploded, not only in films, but also in television shows, commercials, video games, music videos, and much more. Dire Straits' 1984 "Money for Nothing" music video was enormously popular, as its animated CGI character was so different from what the public was seeing in other music videos. Nowadays, it's hard to find any industry that doesn't use digital animation in some form, which makes it a promising career to pursue if you have the interest and the talent.

Now that you know where animation has been, let's take a look at where it's going and how you can break into the field.

The minions in *Despicable Me* were created with 3-D animation.

Computer Animation

WORKING IN COMPUTER ANIMATION: THE BIG PICTURE

1

A s discussed in the Introduction, computer animation really began in the 1960s. However, it did exist in some earlier forms, such as in the 1820s, when the thaumatrope was invented. The thaumatrope is simply a two-sided card, such as an index card, with a picture on each side. A hole is punched on each side of the card, and two handles are created (such as using rubber bands). Those handles can be used to spin the card quickly; when you do so, the images on each side blend and appear to be one moving picture.

In the 1830s, William George Horner and Pierre Desvignes developed the zoetrope, one of the first animation devices. The zoetrope resembled a small carousel. The "drum," or a cylinder with vertical slots cut into it, spun around on a post, and you could place a strip of pictures inside it. You could then look through the slots while the drum spun, and the pictures on the strip would appear to be moving. Interestingly, if you looked over the top of the

The thaumatrope was invented in the 1820s.

open drum at the strip of pictures, you would only see a blur. You had to look through the slots to see the moving images. When the drum is spun, the slots create a strobe effect with flashes of light and dark. You must have the moments of dark between the flashes of light to be able to see the moving pictures.

As you have already read, one of the pioneers of modern computer animation was John Whitney, Sr. Whitney built analog computers and experimented with using them to create drawings and animations. Whitney built his first analog computer from a most unlikely piece of source material: a World War II M-5 anti-aircraft gun director. Using this, he essentially created a drawing machine that was able to control cameras to move above artwork—allowing him to perform the same types of animation functions that would be used decades later on much more advanced digital computers. Inventions such as this that led to Whitney being considered the "father of computer graphics." Whitney's self-built analog animation machines were mechanical in nature, but they were undeniably influential when it came to the development of animation and graphics software for the field of digital animation.

Since then, animation in general has continued to develop and flourish. Further, technology evolves quickly, with changes happening on an almost daily basis, and computer animation is no exception. Today, there are dozens of software packages computer animators use and many career paths within computer animation you can choose to follow. In the next chapter, we'll talk about what sort of software knowledge you'll need, but for now we'll cover the different career possibilities within computer animation.

When computer animation was in its infancy, computer animators were mostly needed for work on feature films and television shows. As technology improved, however, animation became more widespread and job possibilities expanded in other

Mario first appeared in the video game *Donkey Kong,* but he now has his own series of animated games.

areas. Video games exploded in the 1980s and have only gained in popularity in the decades since, as more and more people purchased video-game systems or began playing games online or on their mobile devices. Video games originally used very simple graphics (look at the old *Pong* or *Pac-Man* games for fun), but over the years the animations in them have become incredibly detailed, complex, and even beautiful. The advances in animation for video

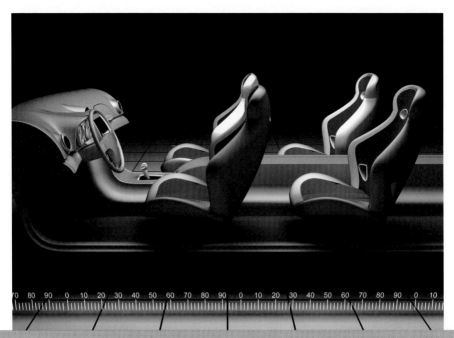

The automotive industry uses computer animation to develop new automobile designs.

games naturally opened up more computer animation jobs in that field, once computers became widely available to the public.

Other industries began to see the power of using animations, too. Ever watch those commercials where a graphic shows a medicine's effect on your body? For example, a side-view of a character with an upset stomach drinks some Pepto-Bismol®, and you watch the smooth, pink liquid go down the character's esophagus and coat his or her stomach, bringing instant relief. That's animation! It may not be the most glamorous of animations, but it's animation nonetheless. The aerospace and automotive industries also began to use animation, to mock up features of cars and planes and see whether they were feasible ideas to pursue. Creating an animation and testing it was much cheaper than building a test car or plane!

> **"** **"**
> *Animating with a computer is like getting both hands cut off and trying to use robotic arms in one of those plastic containers used for handling toxic stuff.*
>
> NIK RANIERI, ANIMATOR ON NUMEROUS FILMS, INCLUDING *WHO FRAMED ROGER RABBIT, THE LITTLE MERMAID,* AND *BEAUTY AND THE BEAST*

Developers of educational software began using animations as learning tools, and when the Internet came along, the field exploded even further. People began using animations on their websites in the form of animated banners or GIFs for clickable links. These animations were typically small and simple, but they were animations nonetheless. Animations continue to be a very real part of the most dynamic sites on the web. Animated GIFs, in particular, are used widely on the web, partly because they are very easy to create. GIF is simply an image format, and an animated GIF is an image that actually stores information for multiple images. These images are then run in sequence to create an animation. They typically loop and play over and over, until the viewer moves on to another page.

Art, Science... and Storytelling?

Computer animation is both an art and a science. You need the technical know-how to work with computer programs, but you also need the artistic sensibility to make creative, aesthetically pleasing designs. However, there's one more piece you need that you might not have considered: the ability to tell a story. You can have the most beautiful, technically correct animation anyone has ever seen, but if you don't have a good story, you've got nothing. You may not be writing the story. If you're working on a television show, a feature film, or even a video game, a script has probably been provided for you. You still need to know the story inside and out, and you need to be able to add details to it in your mind to make it even more real. You need to be able to live in that animated world as if it were real, and to do that you need to know the entire story.

According to veteran animator Angie Jones, whose work has been featured in such films as *The Smurfs*, *Pan's Labyrinth*, *X-Men 2*, and *The Chronicles of Narnia*, "If you think about story while animating, it will give your performance a richness not found in the works of others who are just trying to fulfill the basic needs of a scene. You will be walking in the character's shoes while you animate. You are telling the story through your character's actions. In order for your scene to fit properly into the story, you must understand the character and his or her drive and needs. You also must empathize with the character and those needs, even if you are animating the villain." So add the nitty-gritty details about the character to the story while you animate, in your head, if nowhere else. It will make the character more real to you, and your animation work will be stronger for it.

CAREER POSSIBILITIES IN ANIMATION

Let's talk now about some specific career possibilities in the vast field of animation. Keep in mind that the following animation careers can exist in a number of industries. For example, 3-D modelers aren't only needed in the film industry. They can work in video games, television, advertising, and so on. Although these careers may sound very specific, they are applicable in a wide variety of fields.

Also, keep in mind that any career in computer animation will require both technical skill and artistic talent. However, some jobs are more focused on the technical end of things, while others lean more toward the artistic side. Whatever computer animation job you're ultimately interested in, it won't likely be boring or easy. Computer animation is a tricky business, and the constant changes in the field mean it's always a learning experience.

VISUAL DEVELOPMENT ARTIST

If sketching is your passion, there's a career path in animation for you.

Visual development artists conceive of what the entire animated world in a production should look like, from characters, to backgrounds, to props. They design the overall look and feel of the production. They typically work with the creative departments to ensure that the production retains a **cohesive**, or unified, feel and look throughout. This is typically not an entry-level, or first-time, position; visual development artists have generally worked their way up in the field to that position.

CONCEPT ARTIST

The concept artist works on the initial ideas, creating some of the first visual images that reflect ideas for the project. This position definitely leans more toward the artistic end of the spectrum.

> *" You will be walking in*
> *the character's shoes*
> *while you animate. "*
>
> ANGIE JONES

Concept artists are creative individuals with excellent aesthetic sensibility. They may use computer software to sketch out ideas, but they're just as likely to use pencils or paint, depending on the project.

STORYBOARD ARTIST

Storyboard artist is one of the jobs in computer animation that falls more on the artistic side. Storyboard artists create storyboards, similar to comic strips that basically sketch out what the animated production will look like. They are a crucial part of the team because their designs help guide the entire process. Filmmakers, producers, game creators, advertisers, and other important members of the team will carefully study the storyboards so they can make any important global changes to the production before the actual animation work begins.

Storyboard artists may create storyboards using computers, but they may also create them manually, using pencils or paints. Competition for these positions can be strong, but productions often employ storyboard assistants to help clean up the storyboard artists' work and assist in the process. The storyboard assistant position is typically an entry level one.

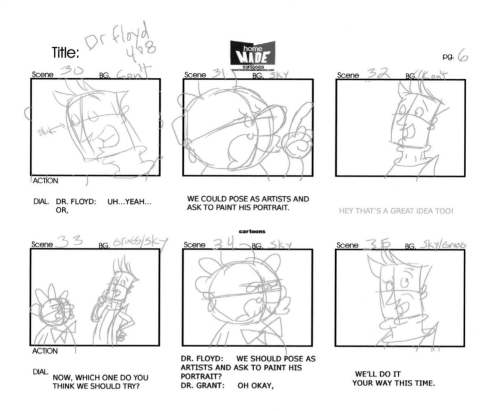

Title: Dr floyd 408

Scene 30 BG. Grant

ACTION

DIAL. DR. FLOYD: UH...YEAH...
        OR,

Scene 31 BG. SKY

WE COULD POSE AS ARTISTS AND
ASK TO PAINT HIS PORTRAIT.

Scene 32 BG. (Kont

HEY THAT'S A GREAT IDEA TOO!

Scene 33 BG. Grass/Sky

ACTION

DIAL.
NOW, WHICH ONE DO YOU
THINK WE SHOULD TRY?

Scene 34 BG. Sky

cartoons

DR. FLOYD: WE SHOULD POSE AS
ARTISTS AND ASK TO PAINT HIS
PORTRAIT?
DR. GRANT: OH OKAY,

Scene 35 BG. Sky/Grass

WE'LL DO IT
YOUR WAY THIS TIME.

Storyboard artists map out the entire production.

ANIMATOR

You're reading a book about computer animation, so of course
there will be a job called "animator." However, it's not quite as
simple as it sounds. There are both 2-D and 3-D animators, as well
as stop-motion animators.

Two-dimensional (2-D) animation is basically "flat" animation
that uses only two dimensions. It's the animation that was used
in early animated films, such as *Snow White and the Seven Dwarfs*,
but it's still used today in many productions. It has become more
sophisticated, and it is now primarily done with computers, but it
still uses only two dimensions.

2-D versus 3-D and CG

Some people think that 3-D animation must be somehow better than 2-D animation, since it introduces a third dimension. This is not necessarily true! No one type of animation is "better" than any other. They all have their benefits and drawbacks. Some animators like working with CG [computer-generated] and 3-D images, but others prefer the "flat" images of 2-D animation. According to veteran rigger Javier Solsona, 2-D has a "kind of freedom that is difficult to reproduce in CG. In 2-D, the artist can draw what he/she wants. He can make use of squash and stretch techniques that are easy to draw in 2-D but hard to duplicate in CG. In CG you are bound to physical restrictions. You can only work on an enclosed, controlled environment. Facial in a character is probably the hardest thing to duplicate in CG. In 2-D, the artist usually deforms the face in ways that are physically impossible."

The Simpsons is one of the best-known examples of recent 2-D animation.

Three-dimensional (3-D) animation, on the other hand, brings in a third dimension to create more convincing animation that appears to have depth and exists in real space. If you've worked with graphs, you know that they have an x-axis and a y-axis. When you introduce a third dimension, you also gain a z-axis. Animation done in 3-D basically uses all three axes to create more realistic images with depth. This is a common trend in current movies, where 3-D glasses allow you to experience the action from another perspective with 3-D films.

Regardless of whether they work in 2-D or 3-D, animators do a variety of tasks, including working on storyboards, creating designs and illustrations, planning narrative sequences, developing technical presentations, and assisting with background design.

The job of animator is highly versatile. For instance, animators work in films and television, advertising, public relations, computer system design, aerospace manufacturing, and web design, and at technical and trade schools.

CHARACTER ANIMATOR

A character animator is a bit more specific than a general animator. Character animators focus specifically on animating characters. They may use 2-D animation techniques,

3-D modeling techniques, or even puppetry to create characters that they can manipulate using various software programs.

CHARACTER RIGGER

A character rigger's job is even more specific. Character riggers use principles of physics, anatomy, and geometry in conjunction with various software packages to make characters move in the most believable way possible. The action of walking seems very simple, for example, but if you stop and think about all of the muscles and bones involved in creating a simple step-taking, arm-swinging walking pattern, you realize just how many intricate movements are involved. Character riggers are experts in these movements and know how to make animated characters simulate them believably. If your skill set lies more on the computing end of things and less on the artistic end, this could be an excellent career option for you, as it requires solid technical knowledge and strong attention to detail.

EFFECTS ANIMATOR

Effects animators are also more specialized types of animators. They work with visual-effects supervisors and the art department to create special effects using compositing tools and 3-D lighting and effects. Effects animators must have strong technical knowledge about the software packages being used on the production.

FLASH ANIMATOR

A **Flash** animator is another specialized type of animator. Flash animators specifically create Flash animations for websites, banners, multimedia presentations, educational software, and video games, and typically don't work on feature films or television programs.

FORENSIC ANIMATOR

This may be the most specialized animator job description of all. Forensic animators recreate crime scenes and accidents to help assist the legal process. They must work with police officers,

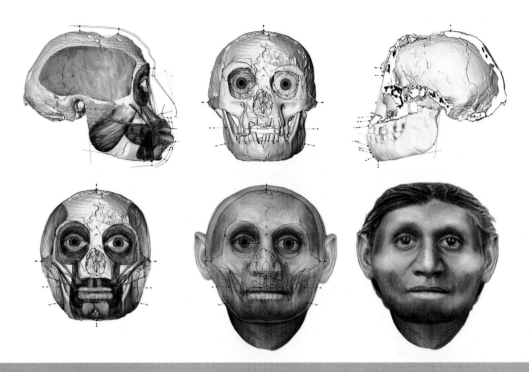

Forensic animators help create accurate renderings of crime scenes, victims, and potential suspects.

forensics experts, and witnesses to the crime or accident to create the most accurate rendering of the crime scene possible.

STOP-MOTION ANIMATOR

Stop-motion is a unique type of animation where models (sometimes made from clay) or puppets are used to create animation. Stop-motion animators create pictures of the models or puppets in various positions, and then use lighting and calculate precise angles to run the pictures together to make what appears to be an animation of the models moving on their own. It likens to the old flipbook animation, where you could take a pad of paper and draw an illustration on the corner of each page, each one just slightly different from the last. You could then flip through the pages quickly, making the drawing appear as if it was moving. Stop-motion animation uses the same basic idea.

Wallace & Gromit is a popular stop-motion animated comedy using Claymation techniques.

If you're having trouble envisioning how such a rudimentary-seeming technique could create interesting animation, consider two of the most popular, relatively recent examples of stop-motion animation: *The Nightmare Before Christmas* and *Wallace & Gromit*. You may have heard the term Claymation, a form of stop-motion animation where the models are made of clay. *Wallace & Gromit* uses Claymation. Each movement a character makes is carefully plotted and arranged by the animator. Later, the movements are pieced together so that the character seems to be moving freely. It may seem like a tedious way to animate, but once complete it can create amazing onscreen effects.

DIGITAL PAINTER

Digital painters digitally paint images created by animators. They add color and clean up the drawing's lines. This is an entry-level position, but one that requires both artistic ability and technical

24

skills, since digital painters need to have a good sense of color and the ability to use various software packages to clean up and paint the drawings.

TEXTURE ARTIST

Somewhat related to the digital painter is the texture artist. Texture artists paint textures on characters, backgrounds, and props. Consider that virtually everything in a scene will have a texture. Bricks are rough and bumpy, skin may have wrinkles or be dry and scaly, animals have fur, automobile tires have tread, trees have bark, birds have feathers, and glass has a smooth, shiny texture. By giving items or characters in a scene texture, the production becomes much more realistic. A dog is more believable if he has soft, shaggy fur or a coarse, wiry coat, depending on the breed.

Texture artists must pay strong attention to detail and be very creative, because sometimes they must imagine what a texture would be if the object or character doesn't exist in real life. An animator working on Pixar's *Monsters, Inc.* reported that the single hardest part of the entire production was animating Sulley's fur. His coat was thick and with such rich and varied color, making it move believably in the breeze or as he walked was extremely challenging.

BACKGROUND OR MATTE PAINTER

Background or matte painters work specifically on backgrounds for productions. They may create entire city backdrops or something much simpler for both animated and live-action films.

The fact that background artists are needed on animated films probably comes as no surprise to you, but you might be more surprised that they're needed on live-action films—the reason being cost and accessibility. Suppose the location of a live-action film is the Parthenon in Greece. The cost of bringing the entire cast and movie crew to Greece for several weeks of filming, plus the difficulty of trying to find a way to shoot a film in an area that is virtually always overrun by tourists, is prohibitive.

Background artists can create rich backgrounds that are later layered behind actors who shot their scenes in front of a green screen.

Some studios choose to build elaborate sets to avoid having to shoot on location. However, more and more often now, studios are choosing to have background artists create detailed and accurate backgrounds of real places, and the actors film the movie in front of a **green screen**. The painted background is later added into the movie, and *voilà*! A movie that appears to be filmed at the Parthenon was actually filmed in Burbank, California, in front of a nice green wall. It's much cheaper and much easier!

LIGHTING TECHNICIAN

You've likely seen background footage of lighting technicians working on feature films or on photography sets. The lighting has to be just right to gain the right look and atmosphere for the shot. However, you might not have realized that lighting is just as important in an animated production. Proper lighting makes an animated scene appear far more realistic. Think about a scene with a character sitting at a table next to a window, showing a bright, sunny sky outside. A lighting technician would rig the lighting in the animation to simulate the bright rays of the sun coming through the window, side-lighting the character, to make the character look as realistic as possible. If that same scene were dimly lit, it wouldn't be at all realistic because viewers could easily see the bright sun through the window and wonder why it wasn't lighting the room.

Lighting technicians need artistic sensibility as well as strong technical knowledge to understand how light bends and fills a room or scene. They work with backlight, key light, fill light, **ambient** light, and more to create realistic scenes. This is also a versatile position, as lighting technicians are needed for feature films, television shows, video games, and even web animations.

INBETWEENER

This unusual job title actually describes exactly what the person does: create the in-between scenes based on a few key scenes provided by the animation department. For example, if the animation department is working on a scene where a character is pitched a baseball and hits it, and then the ball is caught by an outfielder visible in the same scene, the animators might provide a scene where the pitcher is about to release the ball, a scene where the batter's bat is making contact with the ball, and a scene where the outfielder is catching the ball in his glove. From that, the inbetweener must animate all of the scenes in between—from the pitcher's release, to the ball flying through the air, to the batter's movements as he swings the bat, to the ball's movement through the air as it flies toward the outfielder. This process is called **tweening**, and although it sounds complicated, it's actually an entry-level position. Inbetweeners use various software packages to help animate characters' movements when getting from Point A to Point B, provided by the animation department.

MATHEMATICAL MODELER

Looking to make a lot of money in computer animation? Then head for a mathematical modeler position. They earn some of the highest salaries in the field. What's the catch? You'll likely need a Ph.D. in math; most employers will require it, though some will accept a master's degree. You'll need strong math skills to use mathematical equations to calculate the movements required to create 3-D representations of actions, or in other words, simulations. Mathematical modelers use complex math to help simulate movement and action. It's all about the technical details, but if you can do it, you'll be well paid.

COMPOSITOR

Compositors, or compositing artists, are crucial to the production process. They use compositing strategies and software to create the final finished animation with a balanced, cohesive look. Many animations, particularly in feature films, are the result of work by many people, and it's the compositor's job to make the finished product look like the same person created the entire thing. Compositors are also error-checkers. They look for errors in the animation that may have been inadvertently introduced by other departments. The compositor is another animation-team member who works more on the technical side of things than the artistic end.

ART DIRECTOR

Art director isn't an entry-level job. Most art directors have worked their way up from starting as entry-level artists or designers. This is one of the best-paid positions in the industry, and it takes time and dedication to work through the ranks to this position. The art director develops designs and reviews materials submitted by animators, illustrators, and graphic designers, offering feedback for revisions. They may also direct the work of writers, depending on the project. In some productions, the art director may also manage layout.

ANIMATION DIRECTOR

Animation director isn't an entry-level job either. In fact, it's one of the top jobs in the field. You won't walk into it right out of school as a fresh-faced computer animator. Rather, you'll work your way up, first as an animator and then as a key animator who helps manage the animation process. The animation director recruits and manages the entire animation team, reviewing all work done by the animators on the team. This person is essentially the boss of the team and works closely with the director of the production. Animation directors may be **independent contractors**—once a project is finished, their work is done.

FILM AND VIDEO EDITOR

Film and video editors review the animation footage, select the best scenes, and splice them together to create a finished production that runs smoothly and seamlessly. This job in the animation field has a lot of flexibility in that virtually every type of production will require a film and video editor, from feature films to television shows, to advertisements and websites, to video games, and more.

WORKING IN ANIMATION TODAY

These days, computer animators generally work in an office. However, advances in technology and the widespread availability of animation software packages and powerful home computers capable of doing animation work means that if the production team is agreeable, computer animators may be able to work from home. Some productions prefer to have animators working in house, to enable easier collaboration with other departments.

Long work hours are not uncommon when deadlines are approaching. Computer animators have been known to put in crazy hours trying to get an animation just right. We'll talk more about a typical workday in Chapter 3. However, before that, you should know more about what skills and education you'll need to get that perfect animation job.

You'll need training and education to create elaborate animations like this one.

2 STARTING OUT: SKILLS AND EDUCATION

omputer animation is a field full of highly specialized jobs and creative, talented people with a lot of training and background in their chosen area. If you're interested in a career in computer animation, it's a good idea to start planning for it now and put some thought into what specific areas interest you and how you can earn a coveted spot in the field. This chapter will outline some factors to consider—the classes you'll take in high school, what you'll major in, and the college or trade school you'll choose. We'll also talk about the types of software you should become familiar with if you're interested in a career in computer animation.

HIGH SCHOOL

At most high schools, you have to fulfill core requirements, but then there is a little room in your schedule for electives, or classes

> **"** **"**
> *Animation offers a*
> *medium of storytelling*
> *and visual entertainment*
> *which can bring pleasure*
> *and information to people*
> *of all ages everywhere in*
> *the world.*
>
> WALT DISNEY

in different subjects that you choose to take. The electives are what you'll be most interested in if you're trying to prepare for a career in computer animation, but the core classes are important as well. You should strive to do well in your math classes, because the "computer" part of computer animation requires a certain level of math proficiency. Math is especially important if you're striving to become a mathematical modeler or even a rigger. The software programs involved in these positions typically use mathematical concepts and equations to help you animate a character's or object's movement.

Your English classes will be important, too. Getting a job is half the battle, and if your résumé and/or cover letter are lackluster, or worse, full of errors, you aren't likely to get an interview. You'll need to be able to present yourself well to earn a spot in this competitive field, and being able to craft a clean, strongly worded résumé and cover letter is the first step.

High school also gives you chances to take electives. If your school offers classes in art and computer science, by all means take them. For one thing, this is a good way to determine whether you have talent in either or both of these areas, and whether they are something you truly enjoy. You might think you'd enjoy tinkering on a computer all day, but if you take a class on computer science and realize that you actually find the work incredibly tedious, you might want to rethink your career goals. Similarly, you might enter an art class thinking you eventually want a career as a background painter, but then find that you actually prefer working with more three-dimensional materials, in which case you might switch your animation focus to creating models for claymation productions.

Like working in a 3-D medium? Then claymation may be the best path for you.

Also, consider what areas in the field of computer animation interest you. Do you want to work on feature films, or are you more interested in creating animations for the aeronautical, architectural, or automotive industries? If yes, you might want to investigate whether your high school offers courses in **computer-assisted design (CAD)**.

If your high school doesn't offer electives in the areas that interest you, you might investigate community colleges in your area and see whether any of them have classes in your area of interest. High school students can often enroll in classes at community colleges. The credits you earn while there might even transfer over to the college where you eventually seek your degree. You can also look for online classes in your areas of interest. More and more universities are starting to offer courses online, and you may be eligible to enroll depending on the program's requirements.

COLLEGE

No matter what field you're interested in, choosing a college is a big deal. There are literally hundreds (if not thousands) of options, and each offers benefits as well as drawbacks. At a minimum, you should consider program cost, geographical location, courses offered in the program, and the program's quality. Each person has criteria that are important to him or her when choosing a school—only you know the factors most important to you—but you'd be remiss if you didn't at least consider those four features.

The first factor to take into consideration is what type of degree you ultimately want to earn. Two-year associate's degrees in animation are available, but you may find your job options limited with such a degree. The U.S. Bureau of Labor Statistics states that most jobs in animation require you to have at least a bachelor's degree. So while there is certainly appeal to only having to do two years of school after you graduate from high school, keep in mind that this option may limit your chances to get your foot in the door of the computer animation industry.

Another option is a four-year degree. Depending on what part of the computer animation field you want to go into, you might look at the following bachelor's degrees:

- Fine arts
- Animation (computer or classical)

- Game design, development, or programming
- Graphic design
- Digital cinematography
- Film (often with an animation focus)
- Visual effects
- Computer science
- Computer graphics
- Commercial graphics
- Illustration or drawing
- Painting
- Sculpture
- Industrial design

Don't be overwhelmed. The most important thing is to get a degree so you can get your foot in the industry door. Once you have some experience in the industry, there is typically room to move to other positions, especially if you couple that experience with a bachelor's degree in some related field. For example, suppose you major in computer science because you think you'll prefer one of the more technical jobs in the field. However, once you start working in the field, you realize that what you really want to do is be a background painter, which typically requires a type of fine arts degree. If you have artistic talent and some connections in the industry, chances are you can work your way into a position as a background painter, despite your more tech-focused degree. The degree is the key; without it, your options will be far, far fewer.

When you're exploring universities, there are several factors you want to keep in mind. Program cost, courses offered, reputation, and location are a few. Cost is a big one for many people. Art schools can be excellent places to study for degrees in this subject area, but they are expensive. However, public universities are continuing to increase in cost, too, and there

typically aren't as many—or as lucrative—of financial-aid options available at public schools as there are at private ones. So don't discount a private art college if everything else about it is a good fit for you. Investigate what sorts of financial aid might be available to you. You might actually find out you can get a less expensive education at a private college than you could at a public one, depending on the assistance for which you qualify.

Consider, too, the courses offered at the colleges you're considering. Some schools are on the cutting edge as far as offering classes on what's new in the industry, whereas others lag a few years behind. You may find that your prospects when you graduate are better if you've attended a school that keeps up with the most current industry trends. Animation is a rapidly changing field, and you don't want to waste your time earning a degree based on outdated technologies.

You also want to make sure that the degree program at the school you're considering offers a good mix of classes. To be successful in computer animation, you need both computer and art skills. You may be stronger in one area than another, and that's fine, but you do need some of each. You'll need a school

Computer Animation

The Value of that Piece of Paper

It is valuable to earn a college degree in any subject! If you know exactly what you want to do and you pursue a degree in that subject area, great. If you're not sure what you want to do, earn a degree in an area that is at least of some interest to you. It is true that many, many employers won't even talk to you if you don't have a degree. However, if you have any sort of degree, they're suddenly more interested. Your degree might not even be the one they're looking for, but they'll likely be willing to talk to you if you have that nice piece of paper called a college degree.

Even if you ultimately end up working in a completely different field than you first envisioned, having a university diploma will serve you well. It shows dedication, determination, and discipline, among other traits. Moreover, once you have some work experience and a degree, it's fairly easy to move around in industries. Want a real-life example?

My husband is an editor, and his boss is a senior editor, for a pharmaceutical company. However, his boss's degree is in archaeology, of all things! He just got tired of archaeology and the travel involved, and was good with words, so he decided to move into prescription-drug-regulations editing instead. Did it matter that his degree was in something totally unrelated? Nope. What mattered was that he had a degree in some subject, a good work record, and an aptitude for the field he wanted to enter. This is pretty common in the working world. It's a bit of a joke how few people actually end up using their degree in the field in which they originally envisioned themselves working.

If you're interested in a career in computer animation, get some type of degree in the field, but don't worry too much if your interests change as you move along. It happens, and life is flexible.

with a program that will cover computer skills and technology, as well as design, storytelling, and how to draw.

Reputation is always a factor when considering schools. In a perfect world, it wouldn't matter; a degree from No Name University would be just as well regarded as one from an Ivy League school. However, that is not the case. If you attend a school with a good reputation in a particular field, you will get more notice after you graduate. In the field of computer animation, the top three schools in 2013 were California Institute of the Arts (CalArts), University of California, Los Angeles (UCLA), and University of Southern California (USC). You've probably heard of UCLA and USC, as they are big-name universities in many fields, but CalArts may be a new one for you. It's located in Valencia, California, and it is currently the top-ranked school for a degree in animation, according to Animation Career Review. Four of the ten films at the 2013 Academy Awards nominated for Best Animated Feature and Best Animated Short Film were created by alumni from CalArts. If you earn a degree from one of those three universities, people in the industry are likely to notice that on your résumé, and look favorably upon it.

If the top schools aren't an option for you, all is not lost! Research the schools you're interested in and see what their alumni have gone on to do. Most schools have a page on their website that mentions notable alumni, and if they don't, you can likely ask an admissions counselor for such a list. See what the schools' graduates have gone on to do. Not every successful, talented animator has come from CalArts, UCLA, or USC. Plenty have come from other colleges and done well for themselves.

This is actually good information to keep on hand for after you graduate, too. Say you want to apply at Pixar, and you know that six alumni from your university went on to work there. If you can make contact with any of them, it may be a good way to get your foot in the door. **Networking** is key in any industry, and knowing where your fellow alumni have ended up can benefit you.

Location matters when you're considering where to get a degree in the computer animation field. CalArts, UCLA, and USC are all located in Southern California. Animation Career Review describes Los Angeles, San Francisco, and Orlando as "animation and game design meccas" and notes that students who earned their degrees in those three areas appeared to have a distinct advantage over students in other geographical areas when it came to getting internships, networking, finding freelance opportunities, and getting part-time work. New York City, Chicago, Austin, and Seattle were also listed as secondary cities where there are many networking and career opportunities for people in the computer animation field.

THE TRADE SCHOOL OPTION

If a four-year degree just isn't in the cards for you for whatever reason, whether from lack of money, lack of time, lack of interest, or lack of opportunity, there is another option. You can also attend a trade or technical school. These differ from four-year universities in that they often don't require you to take all of the general education prerequisites that universities require. You may earn a degree, a diploma, or a certificate, depending on the program. Be aware that the degree you earn may not be the same as a bachelor's degree from a four-year university. Some trade schools, such as Full Sail University in Florida, offer full bachelor's degrees, but others offer various certificate programs, and those certificates may not be as widely accepted in the industry as a traditional bachelor's degree.

Also, don't expect that a trade school will be less expensive than a university. Some are, when you consider that the program can often be completed in fewer than four years. Others, however, are every bit as expensive as a university.

If you're interested in a trade or technical school, by all means explore them. Research carefully and make sure that the degree or certificate you're working toward will be valuable in the long run. You don't want to invest several years of hard work and money only to discover that your certificate really doesn't get you much in the industry. Just as you would with a university, try to find a list of alumni from the trade school and see what they have done after graduation. That can be a good indication of whether the degree will be useful to you.

Also, be sure to check the **accreditation** for any trade school (or college or university) you're considering. If a school is not accredited, you probably don't want to waste your time pursuing any type of degree or certificate there. It may be time and money wasted on your end.

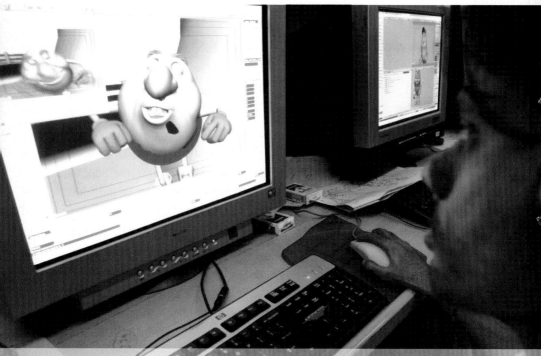

There are numerous software packages used in the computer animation industry.

SOFTWARE PACKAGES

So now that you know about the types of schools and degrees available for the field of computer animation, let's talk about the skill set you'll need to enter this challenging and competitive field.

Computer Animation

The Value of an Internship

Many companies offer internships to students or recent graduates. An internship is a short-term employment opportunity that may be paid or unpaid (though unpaid is more common). Most internships last for less than a year, with three to six months being a fairly typical length.

Although most internships are unpaid, they can be incredibly valuable networking and learning opportunities.

Many of the big animation studios, including Pixar, Disney, Sony Pictures, DreamWorks, Nick Animation Studios, and Blue Sky Studios, offer internships. The details of the internships vary, but one thing is true in any internship: it can be a great way to network.

If you're lucky, your internship will involve you getting some real, hands-on experience in your field. However, it's not uncommon for an internship to involve a lot of busywork, such as getting coffee, making copies, running errands, and so on. Still, you'll get out of an internship what you put into it. Even if you're just getting coffee and making copies, you can meet people working for the company and start making some contacts. If you prove yourself to be a hard worker and eager to learn, those same people may be willing to act as a reference when you start applying for jobs. If you're really lucky, those same people might have some influence and help you land your first job.

If you can land an internship, and you have the time to do it, by all means do. As long as you take the opportunity seriously and put forth your best effort, it can only help your chances of getting a job in the field down the road.

First, you'll need to have aptitude in the field. Maybe you have artistic talent. There are a number of specific jobs in the computer animation field where that will come in handy. Maybe your strengths are more in science, or perhaps you're a computer whiz who loves video games. There's a place for you in computer animation, too. The video game industry is constantly growing and evolving, and there's a place for programmers, game developers, and game designers.

Whichever end of the field you enter, you're likely to need at least basic skills with some software packages, and the stronger your skills, the better your chances of getting a job. However, there is something to be said for on-the-job training, and if you prove yourself to be a quick learner who has an aptitude for computer software, many employers will be willing to train you to use the software they use in-house.

There are classes available for many popular software packages. Take a look at your local community colleges and universities to see what's available. Sometimes parks and recreation departments even offer short classes. Another option is to simply purchase the software (or download a free trial— many software companies offer free thirty-day trials of their products, although some offer limited features until you actually purchase the product) and play around with it on your own. A lot of these software packages are actually quite easy to use once you poke around for a while and experiment.

Animation Career Review considers seven animation packages to be "worth knowing" if you're looking to enter the computer animation industry. Each software package offers different features and is useful in a specific part of the industry. If you're interested in 2-D animation, for example, they recommend Adobe Flash and DigiCel FlipBook. FlipBook has been an industry staple for more than fifteen years, and Flash is a relatively inexpensive package that is widely used for short animations found on the web.

Blender is free. This 3-D animation software is very popular and has a huge web community that boasts numerous free classes

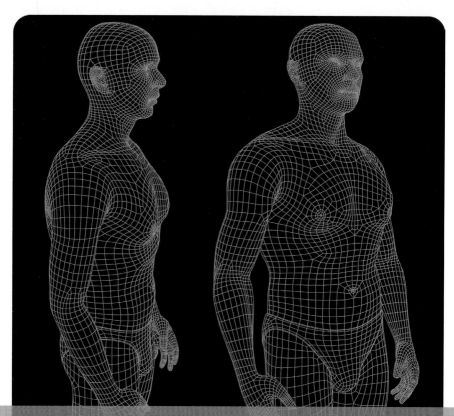

Poser comes with a free library of human and animal meshes.

and tutorials. Poser is another 3-D animation package. It's not free, but it does come with a free library of human and animal **meshes**. Meshes are images made of a network of virtual threads or wires that you can use to practice your animations.

    If you need more features and power than you'll find in Blender or Poser, you can try 3ds Max. It's the industry biggie, but it also comes with a big price tag (several thousand dollars). If you can afford it, try it. If not, play around with Blender and Poser. When you get the opportunity to use 3ds Max at school or through your employer, take advantage. Maya is another 3-D animation program that used to be a competitor to 3ds Max, but now both packages are owned by Autodesk. However, the packages do slightly different things (and Maya is slightly less

You may not need to haul around a giant physical portfolio anymore, but you'll need a good digital portfolio to showcase your work.

expensive), so if you have access to them, it's worth playing with both to see which one suits your needs best.

A newer entry into the field is MAXON's CINEMA 4D. It has been widely used in the film industry in the past five years and is rapidly becoming quite popular. However, like 3ds Max, it comes with a very high price tag in the thousands of dollars.

There are certainly plenty of other software packages out there, such as Anim8or, LightWave 3D, MilkShape 3D, and Adobe After Effects, but this should give you a place to start. If you're interested in a particular job in the industry, poke around on the Internet and see what kinds of software packages companies are using in that role. Then see whether you can get a free trial copy of the software so you can play around with it.

YOUR PORTFOLIO AND DEMO REEL

As you're working toward a career in computer animation, always keep your portfolio in mind. When you finish your education and enter the working world, your portfolio will be a big key to successfully landing a job.

You can build your portfolio while you're getting your education. Ultimately, it should contain your best work, character sketches, paintings and/or illustrations, figure drawings, graphic design work, and **motion studies**. How do you choose what to include in a portfolio? One good way to get ideas is to look at the portfolios of others. See what types of work they've included to give you ideas of what pieces of your own work would be valuable to showcase to potential employers. Alternatively, you can take classes on building a portfolio. If one is offered at your school, it's a good way to start building an impressive portfolio.

A portfolio is usually made up of static images. Since you want to work in animation, you want to show what you can do to make things move. That's where a **demo reel** comes in. Your demo reel is where you can show off your strongest work. A standard demo reel will usually include a title sequence, 2-D pencil tests, a character's walk cycle, a scene that demonstrates a camera move, a space scene, a scene in progress, and a closing sequence. In general, your demo reel should run no more than about four minutes and begin with your strongest work.

Just like it's best to customize a cover letter for a specific employer, it's best to customize your demo reel for the employer you're hoping will hire you and the position you aspire to get. For example, if you are looking for a job in lighting with a studio whose work features an impressive use of lighting, then your demo reel should include the best examples of your lighting work.

It's also a good idea to include a demo-reel breakdown with your demo reel. This consists of notes (within the finished demo reel) that tell what you did on any given piece you're showcasing. If you show an animation of a cat and a dog chasing each other, the demo-reel breakdown frame should tell what you did on that animation. Did you model both of the animals? Did you animate them or do the lighting, shading, or rendering? The studio will want to know exactly what you did on anything you include on your demo reel.

Finally, make sure to keep your demo reel up to date. The field of animation changes rapidly, so your demo reel should include clips that show new ideas and techniques. It shouldn't be full of animations that look as if they were done ten years ago.

THE BIG NAMES

You've learned a lot about what it takes to be a computer animator. Does it sound a bit daunting? It shouldn't. Like any career, it just requires the right mix of talent and determination. Plenty of people have made successful careers in animation, and so can you. Here are just a few success stories.

Veteran animator Tom Sito has been named one of the 100 most influential people in the animation field.

Tom Sito has worked on numerous classic Disney films, including *The Little Mermaid*, *Beauty and the Beast*, and *The Lion King*. He left Disney in 1995 to help set up the DreamWorks Animation unit, where he worked on several films, including *Shrek*. Tom has worked on feature films, short films, television shows, and commercials. He's also a well-known industry lecturer and author, as well as a professor of animation at USC and UCLA. In 1998, *Animation Magazine* named him one of the 100 most important people in animation.

Fred Raimondi is considered to be one of the top digital artists today. His early work on *The Twilight Zone*, *Max Headroom*, and the first season of *Star Trek: The Next Generation* set a high standard for electronic visual effects compositing. In 1993, he moved into commercials at Digital Domain. Among Fred's other accomplishments, he has won numerous Clio awards, an MTV Video Music award, and a Grammy.

Don Waller is an industry veteran who has worked in animation for more than thirty years, doing primarily 2-D and stop-motion work. He began his career in Pittsburgh, Pennsylvania, but after assembling an impressive demo reel during a five-year stint in Iowa, he landed a job in California. Since then, Don has animated numerous music videos, children's films, TV commercials, and feature films including *Jurassic Park* and *RoboCop 1* and *2*. He was nominated for an Emmy for his animation direction on a Discovery Channel program titled *When Dinosaurs Roamed America*.

Larry Weinberg won an Academy Award for his work on *Babe*.

Larry Weinberg is another industry veteran, having worked in computer animation production since 1983. Since then, his animation and software work has helped him win four Clio awards, an Emmy for special effects (for work on *Star Trek: Deep Space Nine*), and an Academy Award (for work on *Babe*). Larry was also a creator and lead developer on the Poser software team.

The Nightmare Before Christmas is a stop-motion animation classic.

Computer Animation

3 ON THE JOB

There are so many different parts of computer animation that it's difficult to describe a typical day on the job. A typical day for a rigger looks very different from a typical day for an animation director, for example. We can, however, explore the general life cycle of an animation project and discuss how various people are involved in each step. For the purposes of this book, I'll be describing the general workflow for an animated feature film, short film, or television production. Animations created for the web or for corporate products will follow a similar workflow, though the process likely won't be quite as involved because the final product is usually shorter.

THE THREE PHASES OF PRODUCTION

Generally, an animation project will go through three main phases of production: preproduction, production, and postproduction.

> **"** **"**
> *Animation is the only thing I ever wanted to do in my whole life.*
>
> JOHN LASSETER, CHIEF CREATIVE OFFICER OF PIXAR AND WALT DISNEY ANIMATION STUDIOS

These phases may overlap, and people may be involved in multiple steps of the process, but let's examine the general flow.

PREPRODUCTION

Preproduction describes the very beginning stages of the production. This is when the production as a whole is planned. The overall look and feel of it is hammered out, the project's goals are defined, the team is assembled, and so on.

Concept artists create visual images for the production, and the art director and other members of the creative team will review the images and provide feedback for revisions.

This part of the process can last for a long time. It's not unusual for designs and ideas to undergo numerous back-and-forth revisions before the animation team finally comes to a decision. At that point, it's time for the storyboard artists to get involved.

Storyboard artists and their assistants lay out the entire production, scene by scene. Depending on the artist, this can be done digitally or manually. Some storyboard artists prefer to draw their storyboards by hand, but increasingly storyboard artists are using computer animation tools to create storyboards digitally.

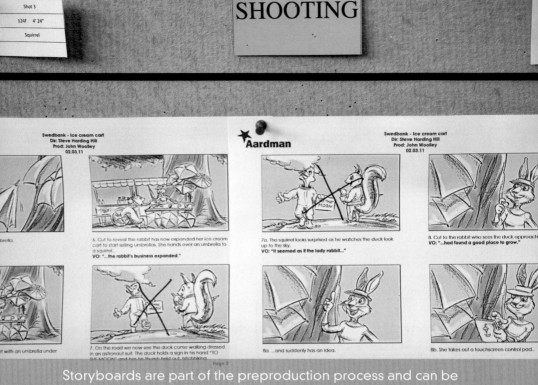

Storyboards are part of the preproduction process and can be hand-drawn or digitally created.

The storyboards are incredibly detailed. The sketches may be rough, but they contain specific information about lighting, object positions, and camera angles. This is necessary because once the actual production process starts, it becomes much more difficult to make changes. The creative team would much prefer to identify potential problems and make changes in the storyboard phase than after the project has already been partially animated. For this reason, this part of the process also involves a lot of back-and-forth, while the art director and creative team review what the storyboard artists have created and provides feedback for any changes.

The finished storyboards serve as a guide for the rest of the production. They ensure **continuity** and cohesion in the finished production. Once the storyboards are finalized and approved, it's time for the background artists to get started creating backgrounds.

Background artists start their work during preproduction, though they often continue to refine backgrounds throughout the production phase as well.

Their part of the process starts in preproduction but often continues into production, as they make changes to the backgrounds to fit various scenes.

The background is everything except any moving objects or characters—those will be added in later by various animators. Some background artists create their work on traditional canvases, and that work is then scanned into the computer and converted into digital format. However, many background artists

Computer Animation

Texture artists create incredibly detailed, realistic textures, adding to the authenticity of the final production.

now prefer to work digitally from the beginning, so they create backgrounds with the help of computer software.

Texture artists can be involved in this part of the process, too, creating textures for backgrounds. A grassy field looks a whole lot more realistic if it appears to have the texture of grass, and a tree looks much more like a tree if the bark has the rough, bumpy, dry texture of real tree bark, rather than a smooth brown surface.

Riggers and modelers may also be involved in preproduction. Once the design of a character or object is nailed down, the modelers can create models and puppets for action scenes, and the riggers can start rigging the puppets or characters to make sure they will move appropriately in action scenes. You don't want to be in the middle of animating a fight scene between two characters only to discover that one character's left arm bends backward when he tries to throw a punch! The rigger should take care of any potential issues such as this when he rigs the characters.

> ## " "
> ### *It's interesting when you're trying to create a character in animation. It's really a communal effort.*
>
> STEVE CARELL, ACTOR, VOICE OF GRU IN
> *DESPICABLE ME* AND *DESPICABLE ME 2*

PRODUCTION

The line between where preproduction ends and production begins is a bit hazy. As you've read, storyboard artists, background painters, texture artists, riggers, and modelers actively work in preproduction. However, they may also be involved during production, as storyboards may need to be tweaked, backgrounds adjusted, textures added or changed, and characters given rigging tweaks. However, in general, production can be said to start when the backgrounds and storyboards are finished and the team is ready to add characters and moving objects.

Usually, the production is led by the work of a key animator, also sometimes called a lead animator, senior animator, or master animator. The key animator will create several key scenes in the production, and the other animators working on the project will then imitate the key animator's work. The team will often create simple motion sketches to determine character movement, and when test shots of the animators' work have been approved, the animators will start actually animating individual scenes. In other words, the characters created in the animation software program will be brought to "life."

Inbetweeners will take key scenes created by the animators and develop the in-between frames that turn the entire action into a seamless motion. For example, the key animator may have created an image of the main character standing in a doorway, looking at a desk across the room. The animation team may have then created an image of the same character standing at the desk, as well as an image of him pushing the contents of the desk onto the floor. Inbetweeners will take those three images and use computer software to create the frames in between, showing the character walking from the door, to the desk, and then pushing the desktop contents to the floor in a dramatic flourish.

Computer animation is essentially done in layers. The background is a layer, the characters and moving objects are a layer, and sometimes additional items are added in another layer. When all of those layers are complete and a semi-finalized production is ready, the animation team goes back to tweak the production. Color key artists and background painters will ensure that color is consistent throughout the production. Lighting technicians, who lit scenes earlier in the process, will ensure that lighting is correct and consistent in scenes. Animators and riggers will tweak characters as necessary to ensure that their movements and actions are believable and realistic. Also, as at all stages, the art director and animation director will review and approve each scene and send it back for revision if necessary.

POSTPRODUCTION

When production is finished, it's time for postproduction. Again, there's some overlap in these two phases. People who work in the production phase are often still working on the project in postproduction, making necessary tweaks and fine-tuning things the postproduction team may have brought to their attention.

Can You Hear Me?

Sound has not been discussed in this book because computer animation is a huge topic, and this book isn't long enough to contain every detail about it. If you're reading this book, you're probably more interested in animation than sound. However, if you are interested in sound, there's a place for you in computer animation as well.

When animated films began in the very early 1900s (1906, to be precise), they were silent. However, that changed in 1928, with Walt Disney's animated short film *Steamboat Willie*, which was also the debut of Mickey and Minnie Mouse. *Steamboat Willie* is noted as being the first cartoon to have synchronized sound. It had a soundtrack added in postproduction. Nowadays, it's very rare to have a feature without sound (though one was released as recently as 2011). Thus, when you consider an animated production, you can be assured that there is a need for sound technicians and editors.

Sound technicians make voice recordings of actors that are eventually added to the production. Since the actors usually don't record together—they work alone, in isolation booths—the sound technician will end up with several tracks from each actor involved in the production. Sound editors, on the other hand, piece together bits of those recordings after the animation work is finished to create seamless dialogue in each scene. It's a laborious process, but it results in smooth dialogue in the final production.

There is not just one sound technician and one sound editor on a production, however. There are numerous sound effects editors (who create and edit, as you might expect, sound effects for the production), **Foley** artists (who create ambient sounds in

Steamboat Willie was the first animated film to feature synchronized sound.

a production), dialogue mixers, and other sound technicians on a full-length animated feature film, for example. Pixar's *Up* lists twenty-six people in the sound department on that film, and that doesn't even include composer Michael Giacchino, who won an Academy Award for the gorgeous score.

Computer animation can involve long days sitting in front of a computer screen.

Postproduction is where the editors become involved. They are experts in storytelling, and they look at the finished animated production, determine the best takes of each scene, splice those together, and cut out any unnecessary scenes.

In any type of production (film, television show, book, magazine article), editors are important because they are somewhat removed from the piece and can look at it with fresh eyes. The animation team has been staring at the work for months (or years) and may not be able to step back and see where a scene is unnecessary or not working well. The editors, on the other hand, haven't been as entrenched in the project, so they can look at it and clearly see the best pieces and the parts that should be cut.

Take the earlier mention of the man standing in a doorway, walking to a desk, and sweeping the contents to the floor as an example. An editor might look at that scene and think: "The walking sequence is unnecessary. The audience doesn't need to see how the character got to the desk—they will assume he walked. They just need to see him standing there and then sweeping the contents to the floor." Pace is a key component of good storytelling—if a story plods along slowly, with too many irrelevant details, the audience will lose interest. The editor can look at the production, see where the irrelevant details are, and make cuts where necessary.

A real-life example of this is in Pixar's film *Up*. The plot of *Up* is that a cranky elderly man, Carl, wants to fly his house to South America, using balloons. He is joined on this journey by a young Boy Scout, Russell. Filmmakers, however, needed the audience to understand why Carl would want to do this. It is, after all, a rather unusual goal.

The filmmakers knew that the most powerful way to provide the explanation was to keep it short and sweet. So in a scant 4 minutes and 18 seconds, we see a young Carl marrying his beloved wife, Ellie, buying and fixing up a home with her, dreaming of the two having children, and then losing their baby, changing their dream of having a family into a dream of traveling to South America, and then growing older together as life's challenges keep draining their "South America fund." Before they know it, Ellie and Carl are elderly. Carl finally buys tickets to South America, but Ellie falls ill and is hospitalized before he can give them to her. She passes away, having never made it to South America. So now, with mass development and construction going on around their beloved home, Carl decides to move their house to South America by balloon.

That's a lot of story to cover in a little over four minutes. The sequence is pure genius and is known as one of the most moving scenes in modern animation. Interestingly, it also contains no dialogue; it is silent except for composer Michael Giacchino's sweet background score. Director Pete Docter says that they originally intended to have dialogue and sound effects, but Ronnie Del Carmen, the storyboard head on the film, suggested that it be silent. When Pete and the rest of the team saw the animated scenes set to Michael Giacchino's score, they realized Ronnie was exactly right. The scenes and the haunting music tell the whole story.

Carl and Russell embark on a great adventure to South America in *Up*.

Compositors also step in at the end of the postproduction process. They look at the entire, nearly finished animation and ensure consistency in light and color across the entire production. They use computer programs to help ensure this consistency.

Finally, the sound is mixed to the project. Sound mixers ensure that music tracks, dialogue, and sound effects are mixed seamlessly in the production, each piece starting and stopping at exactly the right points. There's very little that is more distracting in a production than poorly mixed sound. Have you ever watched a television show where the dialogue coming from the actors' mouths didn't match their mouth movements? It's very disruptive and makes it hard to concentrate on the plot. A good sound-mixing team will ensure that this doesn't happen during the production.

The workflow involved in computer animation will differ in each studio or company, and the job titles may vary as well (a key

animator one place may be a lead animator at another studio or a master animator at yet another, for example). The overall process, however, is generally the same. Now let's take a look at the results of all this hard work and examine a few major milestones in the history of computer animation.

MILESTONE PROJECTS

The list of milestone projects in computer animation could fill an entire book, but in this section I'll cover some of the biggies.

1968 Nikolas Konstantinov and a team of mathematicians and scientists from the Soviet Union created a computer animation of a moving cat. It is thought to be one of the first computer animations of an actual character.

1971 *Metadata*, an experimental 2-D animated short film using the world's first **keyframe animation** software, was released.

1973 *Westworld* was released, marking the first use of 2-D computer animation in a feature film. The film used **raster graphics**.

1976 *Futureworld* was released, marking the first use of 3-D computer graphics in a feature film. They were used to animate a hand and face.

1977 The incredibly popular *Star Wars: Episode IV* was released, using an animated 3-D wireframe graphic to depict the Death Star's trench for training Rebel Alliance pilots.

1978 *Superman* was released and was the first film to use a computer-generated title sequence.

1981 *Looker* was released, featuring the first CGI human character.

1982 *Star Trek II: The Wrath of Khan* was released, making use of groundbreaking new techniques in animation, including fractal-generated landscapes and particle-systems techniques.

1982 *TRON* was released. Many believe *TRON* to be the first use of computer animation in feature films, but you can see that several films preceded it. However, *TRON* is noteworthy for featuring the first long sequence (fifteen minutes) of full 3-D CGI. It also featured very early facial animation.

1984 *The Last Starfighter* was released, featuring the first use of CGI intended to represent real-world objects.

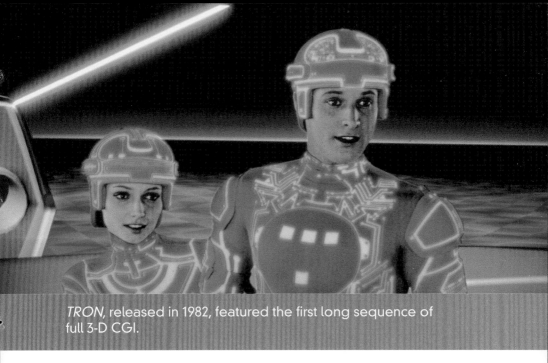

TRON, released in 1982, featured the first long sequence of full 3-D CGI.

1984 *The Adventures of André and Wally B.* was released. This Lucasfilm production is important for being the first all-CGI animated short film.

1985 *The Black Cauldron* was released. This Disney film was the first animated full-length movie to use CGI effects. It was also Disney's first animated film to receive a PG rating. Interestingly, it is also one of Disney's few failures—it was a critical and financial flop.

1985 Dire Straits released the music video for their song "Money for Nothing"—it was the first computer-generated music video and was considered groundbreaking when it aired on MTV.

1986 *Labyrinth* was released, marking the first realistic CGI animal.

1986 Pixar's *Luxo Jr.* was released. It is notable for being the first Pixar film. It was also the first CGI film to be nominated for an Academy Award. Finally, it marked the first use of shadows in CGI. The film was made with Pixar's own RenderMan **application programming interface** (API), which has been widely used in the industry.

1988 *Tiny Toy* was released and was the first computer-animated short to win an Academy Award.

1991 *Terminator 2: Judgment Day* was released, featuring the first use of realistic human movements on a CGI character. It also marked the first time a personal computer was used to create 3-D effects for a major motion picture.

1995 *Casper* was released, featuring the first CGI lead character in a feature film. Many believe *Toy Story* was the first feature film to have a CGI lead character, but *Casper* was released six months before *Toy Story*. *Casper* is also the first feature film to have CGI characters interact with live actors in a realistic manner.

1995 *Toy Story* was released, marking the first fully CGI feature film.

1999 *Star Wars Episode I: The Phantom Menace* was released. It was the first film to use CG characters as supporting cast members, standing next to real actors in dozens of shots.

2002 *The Lord of the Rings: The Two Towers* was released. It featured the first virtual actor to win an award. Andy Serkis, who played the virtual character Gollum, won the Critics' Choice Movie Award for Best Digital Acting Performance, in a new category for the awards show.

2004 *Able Edwards* was released. It was the first feature film to be shot completely on green screens. The team used digitally scanned images for backgrounds.

2004 *Sky Captain and the World of Tomorrow* was released, becoming the first feature film to use live actors with all-CGI backgrounds.

2004 *The Polar Express* was released. It's notable for being the first 3-D motion-capture computer-animated film.

2010 *Toy Story 3* was released and ultimately became the first CGI feature film to gross more than $1 billion.

THE BIG PLAYERS

Animator John Lasseter is the chief creative officer at both Pixar and Walt Disney Animation Studios.

So who are the main companies in this dynamic field of computer animation? Let's start with feature-film and television animation studios. Pixar is perhaps the best-known name in animation right now, but Disney is never far behind. In fact, the two are often neck and neck, and which name is bigger at any given moment depends on who has most recently released a popular film. Walt Disney Studios purchased Pixar in 2006, so in the end it's not much of a competition between the two, but they do remain separate studios in terms of what projects they work on and the teams assigned to

The Nightmare Before Christmas was a huge hit for Tim Burton, who has his own animation company.

the work. DreamWorks, too, has been responsible for a number of blockbuster films, as has Sony Pictures Animation.

Blue Sky Studios, Fox Animation, Industrial Light & Magic, Lucasfilm Animation, Nickelodeon Animation, Warner Bros., and Rhythm and Hues Studios may not have the instant name recognition of Pixar, Disney, DreamWorks, or Sony, but they are all also important players in the field. Tim Burton has his own animation company as well, and some major films have come out of his studio, including *Alice in Wonderland*, *The Nightmare Before Christmas*, and *Charlie and the Chocolate Factory*.

Computer Animation

If you're interested in game development, there are a number of major companies in the development business. A Microsoft **subsidiary**, 343 Studios, produces the Halo franchise (having taken it over from Bungie, another major game developer). The producer of *Rock Band* is 3G Studios. Activision has been around since the late 1970s and has produced a number of very popular games. Blizzard is a bit newer, having been established in 1991, but has also produced a number of very popular game series. Epic Games is responsible for the successful *Unreal* and *Gears of War* games series, and Firaxis Games is responsible for the popular *Civilization* series. The company id Software has produced several important game series, including *Wolfenstein*, *Doom*, and *Quake*. George Lucas is never far from the action, either. He's behind the LucasArts game development studio, which produces the *Star Wars* game series. Maxis Software is behind the popular *Sims* series of games. The game development world is vast and has opportunities for computer animators. These are just a few of the major names in the field.

If you're more interested in computer animation in the corporate world, then the opportunities are too many to mention. Many major corporations use computer animation in some way. They may not have large departments dedicated to animation, but the opportunities are there, particularly in engineering.

The same is true for advertising. The advertising field uses computer animation extensively, so it's simply a matter of finding an agency with a need for animators. Likewise for public relations (PR) firms and web design companies.

Are you wondering what you might earn for all this hard work in the field of computer animation? Then turn to the next chapter!

Your earning potential will vary widely in the computer animation field.

4 SALARIES AND BENEFITS

S o now that you know what you need to do to become a computer animator and what your working life might look like, you're probably curious about how much money you'll make. Truthfully, there is no one definitive answer. Your salary depends on the jobs you get and where they lead you. This chapter offers an idea of some typical salaries and benefits in the industry, and explores the pros and cons of working in computer animation.

SALARY

Pay varies widely in the computer animation industry. It is based on what position you're working in, the type of company you work for, and your level of seniority, among other factors. According to the United States Department of Labor's Bureau of Labor Statistics (BLS), in 2012 multimedia artists and animators earned

> *Computers don't create computer animation any more than a pencil creates pencil animation. What creates computer animation is an artist.*
>
> JOHN LASSETER

a **median** pay of $61,370 annually, or about $29.50 per hour. To put this in perspective, the BLS states that the 2012 median annual salary for all occupations was $34,750. Animators and multimedia artists made almost twice as much annually than the average for all United States occupations.

Before you get too excited, though, the BLS indicates that in 2012, the lowest-paid 10 percent of animators and multimedia artists made $34,860. You shouldn't expect to enter the field at that nice $61,370 salary. You'd more likely start working somewhere around the lower $34,860 figure. The good news is, the top 10 percent of animators and multimedia artists made more than $113,470. So this is a field where there is money to be made … if you're willing to work for it!

Another thing to keep in mind as far as salary is concerned is that most computer animation jobs are concentrated in a few major metropolitan areas that happen to have a very high cost of living:

Living in an Expensive Area

Don't underestimate how cost of living affects your income. If you're coming from someplace that isn't known for having a high cost of living, you may be in for a rude awakening when you move to the San Francisco Bay Area to work for Pixar or Lucasfilm, for example. Rents, transit, and food costs may be much higher than where you're currently living. A studio apartment in San Francisco will set you back somewhere in the neighborhood of $2,900 per month. The average rent for an apartment within 10 miles (16 kilometers) of San Francisco is $3,437, according to a June 2014 article on RentJungle.com. Also, rent increases in the area are outpacing those in the rest of the nation by three times.

Renting in a less expensive area near San Francisco isn't much of an option. Not only will you fight unspeakable traffic as you commute to work, the truth is that nothing anywhere near San Francisco is priced much cheaper.

I speak from experience. My husband has a good job in San Francisco, but he has to commute two hours each way for us to afford the rent. Luckily for me, I only commute to the spare bedroom, where I do all my work remotely. If you land a job with Pixar or Lucasfilm or some other company in an expensive area, it will be an excellent opportunity. However, do keep in mind that the cost of living may take a very big chunk out of that nice salary you earn.

The San Francisco Bay Area, a hotbed for computer animation, also happens to have one of the highest costs of living in the nation.

San Francisco, Los Angeles, and New York City. While the salary is pretty good, it won't necessarily go as far as that same amount might in a less expensive region.

Perhaps in all this there is good news, too. The BLS reports that many artists and animators work primarily from home, so you might ultimately be able to live in a less expensive area and make your salary stretch a bit further.

BENEFITS

What sort of benefits you'll be entitled to as a computer animator depends on whether you are working as an in-house computer animator for a particular company or whether you are self-employed and working freelance. If you are working full-time in house, chances are you'll have access to some sort of insurance plan through the studio. However, if you are a freelance computer animator, you're on your own for health and life insurance benefits. This is a significant factor to consider when you're deciding whether to accept an in-house position. You might be surprised by how expensive insurance is to obtain and purchase. The lure of having company-provided benefits can be great.

FREELANCING

It used to be that the business model for nearly any industry was that all employees worked in one company's office. Period. However, with the advances in technology and the fact that high-speed Internet service is available nearly everywhere, along with the rising costs of benefits, this model has shifted. Many companies don't wish to provide health benefits for employees (largely because they are expensive), and they recognize that freelance, or contract, workers can do the same quality work as in-house employees—but without requiring the health benefits and without taking up space in a physical office.

In some ways, working freelance is great. You can wake up, shuffle into your home office in your pajamas with a cup of coffee, and get to work—no sitting in traffic for a morning commute, no spending money on an expensive wardrobe so you look presentable for the office. Sometimes you can even set your own hours when you're freelance. Some employers will want you available during standard working hours, but others simply want you to finish the work by their deadline, and it doesn't matter when you do it as long as it's done on time.

However, there are drawbacks to working freelance. It's easy to get distracted when you're working at home with no one around to supervise you. You might get used to having a lot of downtime at first, since it will take you some time to build up a client base. When you work in a dedicated office or studio for one employer, you have a built-in client base. Your supervisor will assign work to you. When you're freelance, you have to build a client base yourself, and that can be challenging. Todd Rosenberg, a computer animator who goes by the name of "Odd Todd," launched his freelance animation career after one of his animations went **viral** on the web in 2001. His advice is that getting work as a freelance animator is all about networking. Over the years, he says, you build up small networks of people and gain work that way. If you're not a particularly outgoing person, this type of networking can be a bit intimidating.

You may have a lot of slow periods when you're beginning a freelance computer animation career. This also means periods without pay. When you work for a dedicated employer, you get a steady paycheck, but when you're freelance, you get paid when you work. If you don't work, you don't get paid.

THE GOOD, THE BAD, AND THE UGLY

Like any career, working in computer animation has its pros and cons. Unfortunately, there just is no perfect career. However, for every downside, there is an upside. Let's take a look at a few of both.

Animation work is project-driven. You may be hired to work on a specific project, but when it ends, you may not get hired on quickly, if at all, for another. The reality is that sometimes jobs can be few and far between, and there may be times when you'll go without work. This may be especially true as studios outsource animation work overseas, where workers accept lower pay. The field of computer animation is continuing to grow, though at a slower pace than the average for all U.S. occupations. The industry is projected to grow by 6 percent between 2012 and 2022, whereas all occupations are expected to see an average of 11 percent growth over that same time period. There will be jobs, but whether they will be kept in the U.S. or sent overseas for less expensive labor is questionable.

Animation is also like any other big business: some studios succeed and some fail. Not every animation studio is a Pixar or a DreamWorks, cranking out successful projects and bringing in lots of money. Studios do close, leaving people looking for work. However, if you find work in one of the typically successful companies—Pixar, DreamWorks, Industrial Light & Magic, or

Computer animation typically offers in-house job opportunities as well as work-at-home options.

Lucasfilm, for example—there's a good chance that your job will be as solid as anyone's, provided you work hard and become an asset to the company.

Another drawback is that the vast majority of animation jobs are located in just a few areas: Los Angeles, San Francisco, and New York. These are all very expensive places to live, which may be a big factor in your decision of where to accept a job. Are you ready to relocate to one of these expensive metropolitan areas? If so, great. If not, then perhaps you want to think long and hard about whether computer animation is really the field you want to pursue.

Then there's also the "people" factor. Michael Klouda, a computer graphic artist who specializes in modeling for design and animation and runs Klouda Studios, says that the animation industry has a lot of "odd, quirky, egotistical, competitive, and often unpleasant people." He concedes, "You will also work with a lot of great people," adding, "sometimes it's hard to tell the difference."

Veteran animator Angie Jones supports Klouda's view, stating, "Many creative people tend to be independent loners or perhaps are perceived this way, as the levels of concentration involved in the process of animation can be overwhelming at times."

Having worked with animators, I have to agree with Klouda's and Jones's general assessments. I've met some very personable animators, and others who were egotistical. This can be true of anyone in any industry, but keep in mind that animators tend to be an interesting blend of tech-smart and artistically talented. That combined skill set is something of which they can be proud.

Animators can also work long hours often offset by periods of quiet, when they are between projects. It ends up balancing in the long run, but computer animation is definitely not a 9-to-5 job five days a week. Instead, it's a job where you work when you need to work for as long as you need to work. For some people, that kind of inconsistency can be tiring. For others, it leads to the finished product, which is ultimately rewarding and encouraging.

What are some of the pros of working in the industry? To start with, there are a lot of job choices. As you read in Chapter 2, there are dozens of possible career paths in computer animation. Each job is a bit different, and you can find the one that most interests you and focus your efforts there.

Luckily, there is a lot of work in animation, since it's no longer just for feature films and televisions shows. You can work in video game development, for theme parks, for advertising agencies, in virtual reality, in technical and scientific engineering—the possibilities are almost endless. That keeps life interesting, because if you get bored animating in one part of the field, you can explore options in another area that interests you.

While the "people" factor is cited as a negative, it's actually a positive as well. Those same egotistical people tend to be wildly creative and funny, and you can learn something from them and their work. As animator Cathlin Hidalgo-Polvani says, "You just have to play well with others." You can do that, right?

To prepare for a career in computer animation, take computer and art classes, and seize any opportunity to learn animation software.

LOOKING FORWARD TO A CAREER IN ANIMATION

You now know a lot more about what a job in computer animation involves and your options for career paths. Still interested in working in the field? If so, let's recap what you can do now to prepare yourself for your future career.

First and foremost, take art and computer classes where and when you can. Hopefully your school offers some, but if not, you can look into classes available in your community. Even if you can't find specific classes in computer animation, know that any art or computer classes will improve your skills. Getting experience in different types of art media is a good plan. Try a drawing class, a painting class, or a sculpture class. If you can find one, try a graphic design class. See what types of art most appeal to you.

Computer skills are absolutely essential for a career in computer animation.

On the more technical side of things, one thing you'll learn about computer skills (if you haven't already) is that they build on each other. Many software packages work similarly. If you take a class in one type of software, the skills you learn in there will help you learn other software solutions more easily. Any computer experience in general will help you become more comfortable with new machines and new pieces of software as you're introduced to them. If you have a few computer classes under your belt, you're far less likely to stare blankly at the screen when you sit down in front of your first animation software package.

Second, experiment! Get some animation software and start playing around with it. Some packages are free and some offer free trials. Download a copy and just start playing. Sometimes, getting your hands dirty with no formal training is the best way to learn something, but if that idea makes you nervous, then poke around

Computer Animation

for online software tutorials or buy a book on the software to walk you through it. The important thing is that you start learning the tools of the trade.

Also, start building your portfolio and, if you can, your demo reel. These items will be constantly evolving, so as you create new art, you'll likely remove some of your older work in favor of new. However, in the meantime, it never hurts to have started a portfolio and/or demo reel. That way, when you're old enough to legally work, you'll have something to show if you're trying to get an internship or a part-time job in the field.

It's important that you don't neglect your general studies in favor of art and computer classes. The field of computer animation is very competitive, and you'll need good grades and a strong application to get into a good degree program for your chosen area.

Presumably, you're interested in computer animation because it's something you enjoy, so last but certainly not least, have fun! Computer animation is a unique field that balances both creativity and logic skills, so enjoy putting both sides of your brain to work as you create animations!

WHAT'S NEXT?

You'll be finishing up school and applying for colleges sooner than you think. What should you do in the meantime? Play around with animation software as much as you can, and take art and computer classes. Also, just live your life! The key to being a great animator is being able to essentially paint a story, and storytelling is one of the biggest parts of that. The best way to learn to be a storyteller is to experience life. Look and listen to what's around you, and put those pieces together into stories. You may think your life is pretty ordinary, but it's actually full of great story material, as is everyone's. All you have to do is pay attention to the people and environment around you and add the interesting bits to your storytelling toolbox. When you've figured out how to animate, your treasure trove of material awaits!

GLOSSARY

accreditation A validation process that colleges and universities undertake to meet certain general standards to be considered accredited. Getting your degree through an accredited program is important because employers are far more likely to recognize degrees from those institutions than they are to recognize degrees from unaccredited colleges.

aesthetics Principles of beauty, often specifically as they relate to art.

ambient Related to the surrounding area or environment. Ambient sounds are the everyday sounds in an environment, such as the sound of birds chirping or the hum of a washing machine.

application programming interface Also known as an API, an application programming interface is a set of tools that lets software developers create applications.

computer-assisted design (CAD) CAD programs enable users to design buildings, products, electrical systems, manufacturing flows, infrastructures, and, of course, animations.

CGI Computer-generated imagery; CGI images are images created on a computer.

cohesive Closely united or related.

Computer Animation

continuity An unbroken, continuous flow.

demo reel A video presentation designed to showcase your best work to potential schools or employers.

Flash An Adobe software program that allows users to create graphics and animations that will play in the Adobe Flash Player.

Foley Sound effects added to a film in post-production.

graphical user interface More commonly referred to as a GUI (pronounced "gooey"). A GUI is a computer interface that features user-friendly windows, icons, menus, and buttons and can be manipulated by a mouse. Before GUIs, computer users had to type commands in a rather unfriendly black screen.

green screen This is a green background that actors can perform against when a studio wants to drop in the scene background in a separate layer during postproduction.

independent contractor An individual who provides services to a company but is not employed by the company.

keyframe animation A system in which the beginning and ending frames of animation for a scene are drawn. In-between frames are then added to create a smooth transition. The animators who add the in-between frames are called "inbetweeners," and the process is called "tweening."

GLOSSARY

median The middle value in a series of numbers. The median salary refers to the amount at which half of the workers in a particular occupation earned more and half earned less.

mesh In computer animation, a mesh is an image (usually of a person or animal) created out of a series of virtual wires or threads. Skin, textures, clothing, and so on are later added over the mesh to create the character.

motion study A graphical simulation of motion.

networking Connecting with other people to develop contacts in a particular area of interest. Networking is one of the most effective ways to find a job in a particular industry.

raster graphic A dot-matrix data structure that creates an image based on a rectangular grid of pixels.

savvy Shrewd and knowledgeable.

simulation A computer model.

stop-motion An animation technique in which a physical object is captured in various similar positions. The resulting images, when played together, give the appearance of motion.

Computer Animation

subsidiary A company controlled by another company.

tweening The process of generating extra frames between a beginning and an ending animation frame to create a smooth series of movement.

viral In the world of the Internet, if something has gone viral, it means it has been viewed by many people in a relatively short amount of time.

zoetrope A toy from the 1800s in which a series of pictures is placed on the inner surface of a cylinder. The cylinder has slits in it, and when it is rotated, the pictures inside give the appearance of motion.

SOURCE NOTES

INTRODUCTION

(1) p. 8: Campana, Michael, Andrew Constantinou, and Brian Moore, "The John Whitney Biographical Web Site," www.siggraph.org/artdesign/profile/whitney/whitney.html.

(2) p. 8: Yaeger, Larry, "A Brief, Early History of Computer Graphics in Film," www.shinyverse.org/larryy/cgi.html.

(3) p. 8: Lime, Lemon, "Kitty," www.youtube.com/watch?v=0O4mm3hXNgA.

(4) p. 8: Sutherland, Ivan Edward, "Sketchpad: A Man-Machine Graphical Communication System," www.cl.cam.ac.uk/techreports/UCAM-CL-TR-574.pdf.

CHAPTER 1

(1) p. 11: Hayes, Ruth, "Thaumatropes," www.randommotion.com/html/thauma.html.

(2) p. 12: Hayes, Ruth, "Pre-Cinema Animation Devices," www.randommotion.com/html/zoe.html.

(3) p. 12: Holmes, Kevin, "Original Creators: Visionary Computer Animator John Whitney Sr," thecreatorsproject.vice.com/blog/original-creators-visionary-computer-animator-john-whitney-sr.

(4) p. 12: Campana, Constantinou, and Moore, "The John Whitney Biographical Web Site."

(5) p. 15: Jones, Angie and Jamie Oliff, *Thinking Animation* (Boston, Cengage Learning PTR, 2007), p. 131

(6) p. 16: Jones and Oliff, Thinking Animation, p. 57.

(7) p. 18: Jones and Oliff, Thinking Animation, p. 57.

(8) p. 20: Jones and Oliff, Thinking Animation, p. 87.

CHAPTER 2

(1) p. 32: JustDisney, "Walt Disney Quotes." www.justdisney. com/walt_disney/quotes/quotes02.html.

(2) p. 34: Bureau of Labor Statistics Occupational Outlook Handbook, "Multimedia Artists and Animators," www.bls.gov/ ooh/arts-and-design/multimedia-artists-and-animators.htm.

(3) p. 38: Animation Career Review, "2013 Top 100 US Schools for Animation and Game Design," www.animationcareerreview. com/articles/2013-top-100-us-schools-animation-and-game-design.

(4) p. 39: Animation Career Review, "2013 Top 100 US Schools for Animation and Game Design," www.animationcareerreview. com/articles/2013-top-100-us-schools-animation-and-game-design.

(5) p. 42: Fronzak, Tom, "7 Types of Computer Animation Software Worth Knowing," www.animationcareerreview.com/articles/7-types-computer-animation-software-worth-knowing.

SOURCE NOTES

CHAPTER 3

(1) p. 50: Wloszczyna, Susan, "Pixar Whiz Reanimates Disney," usatoday30.usatoday.com/life/movies/news/2006-03-08-cars-main_x.htm?csp=34.

(2) p. 54: Radish, Christina, "Steve Carell Interview: *Despicable Me*," collider.com/steve-carell-interview-despicable-me.

(3) p. 59: Gaita, Paul, "Scene Dissection: 'Up' Director Pete Docter on the Film's Emotional Opening Montage," http://articles.latimes.com/2010/feb/25/entertainment/la-etw-pete-docter25-2010feb25.

CHAPTER 4

(1) p. 70: Coughlan, Sean, "Quick-Draw Artists," news.bbc.co.uk/2/hi/uk_news/magazine/4861742.stm.

(2) p. 70: Bureau of Labor Statistics Occupational Outlook Handbook, "Multimedia Artists and Animators."

(3) p. 71: RentJungle.com, "Rent Trend Data in San Francisco, California," www.rentjungle.com/average-rent-in-san-francisco-rent-trends.

Computer Animation

(4) p. 74: Luber, Mark, "Animator Jobs – Odd Todd Talks Freelance Animation Careers," careersoutthere.com/animator-jobs-odd-todd-talks-freelance-animation-careers-2.

(5) p. 74: Bureau of Labor Statistics Occupational Outlook Handbook, "Multimedia Artists and Animators."

(6) p. 75: "Computer Graphics & Animation." Ask the Headhunter. www.asktheheadhunter.com/industryinsider8.htm.

(7) p. 76: Jones, Angie and Jamie Oliff, *Thinking Animation* (Boston: Cengage Learning PTR, 2007), p. 201.

(8) p. 76: Jones and Oliff, *Thinking Animation*, p. 201.

FURTHER INFORMATION

BOOKS

Finch, Christopher. *The CG Story: Computer-Generated Animation and Special Effects*. New York, NY: The Monacelli Press, 2013.

Furgang, Kathy. *Careers in Digital Animation*. New York, NY: Rosen, 2014.

Glebas, Francis. *The Animator's Eye: Adding Life to Animation with Timing, Layout, Design, Color and Sound*. Burlington, MA: Focal Press, 2013.

Murphy, Mark. *Beginner's Guide to Animation: Everything You Need to Know to Get Started*. New York, NY: Watson-Guptill, 2008.

Sito, Tom. *Moving Innovation: A History of Computer Animation*. Cambridge, MA: The MIT Press, 2013.

Williams, Richard. *The Animator's Survival Kit: A Manual of Methods, Principles and Formulas for Classical, Computer, Stop Motion and Internet Animators*. New York, NY: Faber & Faber, 2012.

WEBSITES

Animation Arena

www.animationarena.com

This site is chock-full of information about 2-D, 3-D, and Flash animation. Learn more about video game design and read book, movie, and video game reviews. For articles on every conceivable aspect of animation, this is the website to explore.

Animation Career Review

www.animationcareerreview.com

This site offers a wealth of information about careers in the computer animation field, including schools and available programs, information about different careers in the animation field, reviews of animation software, and discussions of notable animation firms.

CareersOutThere

www.careersoutthere.com

This website features information about various careers and interviews with a range of industry professionals.

StopMotionAnimation

www.stopmotionanimation.com

This is a one-stop shop for those interested in stop-motion animation. There are message boards, tutorials, information about upcoming events, and videos, among many other resources.

BIBLIOGRAPHY

AMC Filmsite. "Greatest Visual and Special Effects (F/X)—Mile stones in Film." www.filmsite.org/visualeffects9.html.

Animation Career Review. "2013 Top 100 US Schools for Animation and Game Design." Last modified February 28, 2013. www.animationcareerreview.com/articles/2013-top-100-us-schools-animation-and-game-design.

_____ . "Articles Profiling the Different Professional Career Paths in Animation, Design, and Gaming." www.animationcareerreview.com/articles/articles-profiling-different-professional-career-paths-animation-design-and-gaming.

Bureau of Labor Statistics Occupational Outlook Handbook. "Multimedia Artists and Animators." January 8, 2014. www.bls.gov/ooh/arts-and-design/multimedia-artists-and-animators.htm.

Campana, Michael, Andrew Constantinou, and Brian Moore. "The John Whitney Biographical Web Site." www.siggraph.org/artdesign/profile/whitney/whitney.html.

"Computer Animation Schools and Colleges." Trade-Schools.net. Last updated August 6, 2014. www.trade-schools.net/media-arts/animation.asp.

Coughlan, Sean. "Quick-Draw Artists." *BBC Magazine*. Last updated March 31, 2006. news.bbc.co.uk/2/hi/uk_news/magazine/4861742.stm.

Dash, Anand Sager. "Animation Techniques." Arena Animation. www.arena-multimedia.com/blog/index.php/animation-techniques.

DBS Interactive. "What Is the Difference Between 3D and 2D Animation?" Last updated January 29, 2010. www.dbswebsite.com/

blog/2010/01/29/what-is-the-difference-between-3d-and-2d-animation.

Digital-Tutors "Demo Reel Tips." www.digitaltutors.com/11/de-moreel.php.

Erwert, Anna Marie. "S.F. Rents Up More Than 3 Times Higher Than National Average." Last updated January 30, 2014. blog.sfgate.com/ontheblock/2014/01/30/s-f-rents-up-more-than-3-times-higher-than-national-average/#20080101=0&20081103=0&20082105=0.

Fronzak, Tom. "7 Types of Computer Animation Software Worth Knowing." Animation Career Review. www.animationcar-eerreview.com/articles/7-types-computer-animation-soft-ware-worth-knowing.

Furgang, Kathy. *Careers in Digital Animation*. New York, NY: Rosen, 2014.

Gaita, Paul. "Scene Dissection: 'Up' Director Pete Docter on the Film's Emotional Opening Montage." *Los Angeles Times*. Last updated February 25, 2010. articles.latimes.com/2010/feb/25/entertainment/la-etw-pete-docter25-2010feb25.

Hayes, Ruth. "Pre-Cinema Animation Devices." www.randommo-tion.com/html/zoe.html.

———. "Thaumatropes." www.randommotion.com/html/thauma.html.

Holmes, Kevin. "Original Creators: Visionary Computer Animator John Whitney Sr." June 11, 2012. The Creators Project. thecre-atorsproject.vice.com/blog/original-creators-visionary-comput-er-animator-john-whitney-sr.

BIBLIOGRAPHY

Jones, Angie, and Jamie Ollif. *Thinking Animation*. Boston, MA: Cengage Learning PTR, 2007.

JustDisney.com. "Walt Disney Quotes." www.justdisney.com/walt_disney/quotes/quotes02.html.

Klouda, Michael. "Computer Graphics & Animation." Ask the Headhunter. www.asktheheadhunter.com/industryinsider8.htm.

Lime, Lemon. "Kitty." YouTube video, 1:24. November 1, 2010. www.youtube.com/watch?v=0O4mm3hXNgA.

Luber, Mark. "Animator Jobs – Odd Todd Talks Freelance Animation Careers." Careers Out There. careersoutthere.com/animator-jobs-odd-todd-talks-freelance-animation-careers-2.

McLaughlin, Dan. "The History of Animation." The UCLA Animation Workshop. animation.filmtv.ucla.edu/NewSite/WebPages/Histories.html.

National Film Board of Canada. "Metadata." www.onf-nfb.gc.ca/en/our-collection/?idfilm=10954.

Ohio State University Department of Design, The. "CGI Historical Timeline." Last updated November 1, 2003. www.design.osu.edu/carlson/history/timeline.html.

———. "TRON: The 1982 Movie." www.design.osu.edu/carlson/history/tron.html.

Pegoraro, Rob. "Incredibles, Inc: The Story of How Computer Programmers Transformed the Art of Movie Animation." *The Washington Post*. June 29, 2008. www.highbeam.com/doc/1P2-16792932.html.

Pixar. "Creating a Demo Reel." www.pixar.com/careers/Creating-a-Demo-Reel.

Premiumbeat. "Top 20 Tips for Creating a Successful Demo Reel." www.premiumbeat.com/blog/top-20-tips-for-creating-a-successful-demo-reel.

Radish, Christina. "Steve Carell Interview: *Despicable Me*." Last updated April 20, 2010. collider.com/steve-carell-interview-despicable-me.

RentJungle. "Rent Trend Data in San Francisco, California." Last updated July 30, 2014. www.rentjungle.com/average-rent-in-san-francisco-rent-trends.

Rose, Frank. "Kid Robot and the World of Tomorrow." Last updated May 23, 2004. archive.wired.com/wired/archive/12.05/conran.html.

Rosebush, Judson. "A History of Computer Animation." Last updated March 20, 1992. www.vasulka.org/archive/Artists5/Rosebush,Judson/HistoryCompAnimation.pdf.

Sanders, Adrien-Luc. "A Realistic Look at Freelance Animation Work." www.animation.about.com/od/careertips/a/freelanceprocon.htm.

Sutherland, Ivan Edward. "Sketchpad: A Man-Machine Graphical Communication System." University of Cambridge. www.cl.cam.ac.uk/techreports/UCAM-CL-TR-574.pdf.

Wloszczyna, Susan. "Pixar Whiz Reanimates Disney." *USA Today*. usatoday30.usatoday.com/life/movies/news/2006-03-08-cars-main_x.htm?csp=34.

Yaeger, Larry. "A Brief, Early History of Computer Graphics in Film." ShinyVerse.org. www.shinyverse.org/larryy/cgi.html.

INDEX

Page numbers in **boldface** are illustrations.

ABOUT THE AUTHOR

CATHLEEN SMALL is a writer, editor, and teacher living in the San Francisco Bay Area. She has edited hundreds of technical books on computer software and systems, the Internet, music technology, photography, and yes, animation. She has written a number of books for Cavendish Square, including several titles in the Web Wisdom series. In her spare time, Cathleen is an avid traveler and an active participant in the special-needs community. She lives with her husband, two young sons, and two pugs. Her favorite animated film is *Up*.